MASSEY FERGUSON TRACTORS

Jonathan Whitlam

AMBERLEY

First published 2017

Amberley Publishing
The Hill, Stroud,
Gloucestershire, GL5 4EP

www.amberley-books.com

ISBN: 978 1 4456 6724 9 (print)
ISBN: 978 1 4456 6725 6 (ebook)

British Library Cataloguing in Publication Data.
A catalogue record for this book is available from the British Library.

Typeset in 10pt on 13pt Celeste.
Typesetting by Amberley Publishing.
Printed in the UK.

Contents

Foreword

This book is not intended to be a concise history of Massey Ferguson; a much larger volume would be needed to do that. Instead this book is designed to be an overview of the tractors that have bore the Massey Ferguson name from 1957 to 2017 and show how the MF tractor has evolved in that time.

Although I have tried to give a sense of the global nature of the MF tractor operations, inevitably the main part of this book will focus on the British viewpoint and specifications as they are the most commonly seen machines in the UK. Again, a much larger book would be needed to give anything like a full account of every model and variation.

All information is only provided as a rough guide due to the huge variance of specifications and models built on a worldwide scale during the past sixty years and all horsepower figures are also only given as a guide and are taken from contemporary sales literature.

Intended as a retrospect of the history of the Massey Ferguson tractor, all the photographs show machines in the modern era, either in original or restored condition, and therefore various features may well have been altered from when they left the factory. Photographs are by the author, and also Kim Parks, who I would like to thank for making his extensive photographic collection available.

Introduction

Massey Ferguson is one of the world's most famous tractor brands, its name gracing the sides of tractor bonnets for sixty years now. During six decades, the firm has constantly been in the tractor business, although other sides of the company have waxed, waned or disappeared.

Massey Ferguson, as a company, did not come into existence until the big merger of 1953, and even up to 1957, the Massey-Harris name was still used on a range of tractors and machinery, especially combine harvesters. The Massey-Harris business, based in Canada, was itself the result of a merger in 1891, between the Daniel Massey and Alanson Harris companies.

In 1917 Massey-Harris imported the Bull tractor into Canada, a strange looking three-wheel design that was built in the USA. After several other false starts, it was the acquisition of the JI Case Plow Company factory in Racine, Wisconsin that saw Massey-Harris finally get the tractor building facilities it needed.

The first tractor to be sold by Massey-Harris was the very unusual-looking Bull tractor.

The deal included the Wallis tractor design, which became the foundation for the Massey-Harris tractor. In 1945 Massey-Harris harvesting equipment production began in Manchester in England with the Massey Harris 744PD arriving in 1948, based on the Canadian 44 series but powered by a Perkins diesel engine. This became the 744D when production was moved from Manchester to a new facility in Kilmarnock, Scotland.

In 1957 tractor production ceased in North America and finished at Kilmarnock in 1958 with the 745S model. The reason was that, back in 1953, Massey-Harris had merged with British tractor maker Ferguson, bringing into the fold a much more advanced type of farm tractor.

Harry Ferguson hailed from Ireland and was an engineer and inventor, designing a brand-new way of using a tractor, which came to the marketplace in 1936 as the Ferguson Type A tractor. Built for Ferguson by the David Brown company of Huddersfield, the Type A used the Ferguson System of three-point rear linkage and hydraulic draft control. For the first time a mounted implement became an actual part of the tractor itself rather than just being towed behind. The benefits were enormous and went far beyond the ability to lift and lower the implement at the headland to turn, as the three-point linkage design also allowed weight to be transferred to the tractors front wheels if the implement in the soil encountered an obstruction, therefore preventing the tractor turning over onto the driver. The operator could then lift the implement over the obstruction, lower it again into work and off he went.

Unfortunately, although the tractor worked brilliantly, farmers in Britain were still wary of mechanisation and certainly were not impressed by having to not only buy the tractor, but also all the specially produced implements that were needed to go with it to make it work properly. By the late 1930s unsold tractors were mounting up and Harry Ferguson decided to try and come up with a solution after falling out with David Brown over design changes to the Type A. The result was a historic meeting with Henry Ford who agreed to

The General Purpose was built by Massey-Harris from 1930 and was a very advanced design with four-wheel-drive from four equal size wheels.

The Ferguson Type A, introduced in 1936 and built for Harry Ferguson by David Brown in Huddersfield, featured the Ferguson System of three-point linkage and hydraulic draft control.

produce a new tractor incorporating the Ferguson System and the launch in 1939 of the Ford 9N, a tractor that used stylish automotive-type design for the tractor and of course the Ferguson System three-point linkage. This arrangement was again short-lived and in 1946 Harry Ferguson put the Ferguson TE20 into production in Coventry, England using the Standard Motor Company to build it for him. Fitted at first with a Continental petrol engine, this was later changed to a Standard petrol engine with the choice of vaporising oil or lamp oil powered versions. A diesel engine also supplied by Standard was built and there were many variations such as narrow, industrial and vineyard models.

The TE20 was a huge success and gradually evolved into many variations, although all were still based on Harry Ferguson's vision of a lightweight and simple tractor for all farming tasks, and grey remained the colour scheme.

The merger in 1953 of Ferguson and Massey-Harris resulted in the change of name to Massey-Harris-Ferguson, but otherwise things remained unchanged for some time with separate product lines, the Ferguson side concentrating on tractors and the Massey-Harris part continuing with its successful harvester range. It also meant that in the USA the Massey Harris 50, powered by a four-cylinder Continental petrol engine, was also produced as the Ferguson 40 to sell through Ferguson dealers and provide a larger tractor alongside the TE20 derived models.

The grey and gold painted Ferguson FE35 was introduced in 1956 as the replacement for the TE20 and had been largely designed by the Ferguson company prior to the merger. It was powered by a Standard engine that could be fuelled by either petrol, lamp oil, vaporizing oil or diesel, the latter becoming ever more popular at this time, the various fuels giving power outputs between 30 and 37 hp. A six forward and two reverse gearbox gave more gears than the TE20 and revised styling also produced a different looking machine, although at its heart remained the Ferguson System. The new bonnet was very

This is a preserved TEA 20 version of the Ferguson TE20, fitted with a Standard Motor Company-built four-cylinder petrol engine.

The Ferguson TEF 20 was the diesel version of the famous 'little grey Fergie'.

different from its predecessor, however it no longer tilted up for maintenance, instead there were liftable flaps placed in strategic positions on top of the bonnet. Industrial and vineyard versions of the FE35 were built and it was still constructed in the Banner Lane factory in Coventry.

The Ferguson 40 was an American Ferguson development to provide a larger tractor and was also produced as the Massey-Harris 50.

The Ferguson FE35 arrived in 1956, three years after the Massey-Harris and Ferguson merger.

1957 was a pivotal year as Harry Ferguson resigned his position with the company and the Harris part of the name was dropped, leaving simply Massey Ferguson as the company moniker. It was the beginning of a true golden age of tractor building, and this book is the story of that time.

CHAPTER 1

The Red and The Grey

The Massey Ferguson 35, launched in 1957, introduced the Massey Ferguson name onto the sides of a tractor, but under the new badge and the new colour scheme it was basically still a Ferguson FE35.

The power output depending on the fuel used was still 30 to 37 hp, with the petrol and diesel engine versions being the most powerful. The options list was quite extensive and a deluxe version featured a live power take-off and hydraulics. Although not used on the very first MF 35 tractors, a new logo appeared in 1957 for the newly renamed company using a triple triangle motif with the letters MF in the centre. The 35 still used the Standard four-cylinder diesel engine – a good enough power unit when in work, but often very temperamental to start from cold.

The diesel-powered version of the Massey Ferguson 35 was still powered by the Standard Motor Company four-cylinder engine of 37 hp.

The tinwork of the Massey Ferguson 35 certainly stood out more in red than the grey of the FE35.

The TVO version of the 35 remained popular for some time with many farmers who wished to carry on with a fuel that they were familiar with.

At the end of 1957, at the Royal Smithfield Show, a larger tractor joined the 35 in the MF lineup. The 65 was certainly a bigger machine, powered as it was by a four-cylinder Perkins A4.192 diesel engine of just over 50 hp, and the distinctive bonnet styling made it look very imposing, standing out from all that had gone before – at least in Europe.

With the 35 and 65 models Massey Ferguson had a range of tractors to sell through its dealerships. There was also a smaller sister to the 35 in the shape of the 25, built in the French factory in Beauvais and based on earlier French designs. Physically smaller than the 35, the 25 was powered by a 22 hp four-cylinder Perkins A4.107 diesel engine and came with an eight-speed gearbox. Narrow, vineyard and high-clearance versions of the 25 were also built but it was not a popular model in the UK.

So far the British tractors had been built in the Coventry factory owned by the Standard Motor Company but, in 1959, MF took over the leasehold of the site and also bought Perkins, the engine manufacturer based in Peterborough.

The Massey Ferguson 65 was based on the earlier larger North American tractor designs and shared similar bonnet lines with the old Ferguson 40.

13

Perkins provided the motive power for the 65 in the form of a 50 hp four-cylinder A4.192 diesel engine.

The little 25 was built in France and provided a smaller alternative to the 35 with power coming from a four-cylinder Perkins engine of 22 hp.

The Standard four-cylinder diesel engine was replaced in 1959 by a Perkins unit. With this three-cylinder 37 hp diesel engine fitted, the 35 really was a superb tractor, the cold starting issues were resolved and the machine was much easier to use. The engine chosen was the A3.152 unit and the result was also a more powerful 35, with power now just a shade under 40 hp, increasing this already versatile machines usefulness. The transmission gave six forward speeds and two in reverse and vineyard and high-clearance versions were also built as well as industrial variants.

1962 saw a Mark II 65 replace the original model with a more powerful Perkins AD4.203 diesel engine of just under 57 hp, making the new 65 a gutsier performer. Standard and high-clearance models of the 65 were built, as was an industrial version.

It was also in 1962 that the Multi-Power splitter gearbox arrived as an option on the 65, giving twelve forward and four reverse speeds, effectively doubling those available.

At the Royal Smithfield Show in the same year, the Multi-Power gearbox was also made available on a new deluxe version of the 35. Called the 35X, this tractor also had the extra bonus of more power – over 44.5 horsepower to be exact, squeezed from the Perkins A3.152 power unit. For the first time, the 35X was only available with a diesel engine, but the standard 35 was still offered with the choice of either petrol or TVO fuelling.

A bigger tractor than the 65 was also offered at the Smithfield Show in 1962 when the American-built Super 90 was displayed with 77 hp available from its diesel engine, but this proved to be a short-lived offering.

The 35 gained the excellent Perkins A3.152 three-cylinder diesel engine in 1959, which fitted neatly under the existing tinwork.

The words Multi Power written on the bonnet of this 65, seen at a ploughing match in the south of England, identify it as being fitted with the twelve forward and four reverse transmission first seen in 1962.

Narrow versions of the 35 were very common and were designed for work in vineyards, hop gardens and orchards.

The opening middle section of the bonnet allowed access to the radiator and fuel tanks for refueling.

The 35X was a deluxe version of the 35 first introduced in 1962.

The engine used in the 35X was the Perkins A3.152 engine used originally but with fuelling adjusted to get the extra few horses. This engine was very reliable and easily coped with the extra power output.

Industrial versions of the 35X were also offered.

This example of the 35X is a high-clearance version for spraying growing crops.

The 35X makes a fine tractor to take to rallies and shows. Note that the headlights on this one have been raised to accommodate a front loader during its previous working life.

CHAPTER 2

Red Giants to Big Giants

In December 1964 the Massey Ferguson 100 Series was unveiled to the public for the first time and the publicity people had come up with a snazzy name for the new range – the Red Giants.

Four models were introduced, all with brand-new square-type bonnet styling and with a true family look to them, with the front headlights now being built into the front of the radiator grille itself, making a neater overall appearance. They were produced predominantly in the USA, Coventry in the UK, Beauvais in France and, later, a few in Germany.

Smallest of the lot was the little 130, based on the outgoing 25 tractor and fitted with a Perkins four-cylinder A4.107 diesel engine producing 30 hp. It was fitted with an eight forward by two reverse gearbox and also included differential lock and disc brakes in its standard specification. Built in Beauvais, it was also offered in high-clearance and narrow versions.

Underneath the new DX Series tinwork, the 130 was a revamped version of the 25 model and used the same Perkins engine of 30 hp.

Based on the 35, the 135 used the 35X three-cylinder Perkins diesel engine and was rated at 45 and a half horsepower, but otherwise was basically a 35 in new clothes! Originally offered with a standard six forward by two reverse transmission, or the Multi-Power twelve forward by four reverse, an eight-speed gearbox was later fitted as the standard option. There was a bewildering array of different versions of the 135 built for various markets, including petrol powered and narrow vineyard and low orchard models as well as French versions using the Perkins A3.144 diesel engine.

Next up was the 165, which replaced the 65 model and was basically exactly the same as the Mark II 65, but with the new tinwork. Featuring the Perkins four-cylinder A4.203 engine with a rating of just over 58 hp, the 165 was a powerful performer, this engine being particularly sweet running and smooth. Either a standard six forward and two reverse or Multi-Power twelve forward and four reverse gearbox was fitted to the 165 and this tractor was also sold in a high-clearance version. Many different versions of the 165 were built including petrol and tricycle row crop machines, particularly in the USA.

Biggest in the range was now the 175, a 66 hp tractor powered by a Perkins four-cylinder engine. In the USA there were also the 150, 180 and 1100 models and in France the 122, 140 and 145, although the 135, 165 and 175 remained as the core models in these markets as well, with the exception of the 175, which was sold in the USA and the UK but not initially in France.

Most of the Red Giants were sold without a cab to begin with, although the 135, 165 and 175 were often produced with flat-top rear wings to accommodate the fitting of a weather cab. Massey Ferguson did offer a very well-finished weather cab built for them by coach maker Duple, of Blackpool, consisting of a steel frame and fibreglass structure.

The 35X had been a very successful tractor and its successor, the 135, would take that popularity to new heights. Now with 45.5 horsepower, the 135 was an ideal machine for many farmers due to its versatility.

A restored 135 turning hay in Suffolk during the summer of 2016. Many 135 tractors are still used on farms today, especially for jobs such as haymaking, and there cannot be many farms that have not run at least one of these tractors over the years.

As with the 35 before it, the 135 was also produced in a variety of different narrow and industrial versions. This is a vineyard version with low build and narrow width.

The 165 might have featured the mechanicals of the Mark II 65, but the new tinwork made it look completely new.

With 66 hp on tap, the 175 was a large tractor when introduced in 1964 with the rest of the Red Giants range. It also came with a higher standard specification including PAVT rear wheels.

Built in North America the 180 was a powerful machine with 83 hp produced by its Perkins A4.236 diesel engine. It was produced in standard and wide axle versions as well as the tricycle arrangement shown here.

The Massey Ferguson weather cab looked much more sophisticated than competitive manufacturers' examples, but was still very simple. It was made by Duple – a firm more commonly associated with bus and coach bodybuilding.

Pressure Control was a new feature on the options list and was a way of transferring the weight of a trailed implement, or trailer, onto the back of the tractor for better control.

Built in America from 1965, the big 1100 went on sale as part of the Red Giants range in Britain in 1967 and was powered by a six-cylinder Perkins diesel engine of 105 hp, making this the biggest Massey Ferguson tractor so far, and the first to be fitted with the Pressure Control implement weight transfer system from new.

In 1968 the Mark II 165 arrived with 62 hp now available from a Perkins A4.212 engine, while the 175 disappeared from the product list in favour of the 178, with 72.5 horsepower on tap and several other improvements made to the tractor.

Another large tractor arrived in the UK in 1969 in the shape of the French-built 1080, which was originally a 90 hp tractor but was later built in an improved form with 92 horses under its 100 Series style bonnet. Powered by the Perkins four-cylinder A4.318 diesel engine and fitted as standard with a twelve forward by four reverse Multi-Power transmission, the 1080 was designed to be the European flagship for the 100 Series range but failed to live up to expectations. Fitted with a large, but rather noisy, safety cab built by Sta-Dri for the British market, there was also a four-wheel-drive version for some markets, which was rated at a slightly lower 88 hp. There was also an American 1080 using the same engine, which was joined by the 1150 with a AV8.510 Perkins V8 engine producing a mighty 145 hp. The smaller 100 Series tractors were built in both Coventry, Beauvais and in North America, but the larger machines were never built in the UK and the market here for them was also fairly limited.

The 1100 was built in America from 1967 and sold in the UK from 1967. This was a large and powerful machine with the 100 Series tinwork concealing a 105 hp six-cylinder Perkins A6.354 engine.

The 1080 from France was a big tractor with 90 hp available originally from its Perkins four-cylinder engine. Safety cabs for the UK market were sourced from Sta-Dri but proved to be very noisy.

This restored 165 is fitted with the MF safety cab, which used a frame built by Sirocco and consisted of flexible cladding stretched over the metal work to produce a simple, but very effective, cab.

Still at work on a Suffolk farm, the flexible cladding has all but disappeared from this 135, as have both doors as it plants sugar beet.

1970 saw the arrival of the safety cab legislation in Britain, where new tractors had to be fitted with a protective structure to protect the driver from injury in the event of a roll over incident. Massey Ferguson developed a frame with cab builder Sirocco, which was fitted with cladding. The flexible clad cabs were made by Sirocco near Chester, and the rigid version by GKN Sankey, in Shropshire.

1971 saw three new longer wheelbase models arrive and sold alongside the existing models as the 'eight line'. The 148 with its extra length was certainly a luxurious alternative to the 135 with its Perkins AD3.152 engine tuned to deliver 49 hp and with an impressive list of standard features plus the choice of eight-speed or twelve-speed transmission. A narrow version was also built in Beauvais.

The 168 had 69 hp available from its Perkins A4.236 diesel engine and the choice of either the eight-speed manual or twelve-speed Multi-Power gearboxes.

The 185 and 188 models both shared the same Perkins four-cylinder A4.248 engine rated at 75 hp, making this a more powerful machine than the 178 it replaced.

In France a four-wheel-drive version of the 188 was also produced. Four-wheel-drive versions of all of the 100 Series tractors were offered factory fitted in Europe, and Italian firm Selene also offered four-wheel-drive conversions of the 135, 175 and 178 including both unequal and equal size wheel versions. In Britain this was left to an outside firm, Four Wheel Traction, who fitted the Selene axle and drive system from Italy under license and which was often fitted to tractors by the dealer network. The Four Wheel Traction unequal size wheel conversions were built for the 135, 165, 175, 178, 185 and 188 models, and

The 148 was a deluxe version of the 135 with 49 hp now available from the Perkins three-cylinder motor. It also had a longer wheelbase. This pristinely restored 148 from Suffolk would have originally been fitted with a safety cab when new to meet the 1970 ruling on driver protection.

A close-up of the gear selectors on the 148 also show the ignition key for starting and the Multi-Power switch at top centre.

This restored 168 is shown at a ploughing match in the south of England and is powered by a 69 hp Perkins A4.236 engine, which made it a superior tractor to the standard 165.

This 168 is fitted with the rigid clad cab built for MF by GKN Sankey, which gave more comfort but was also rather harder on the driver's ears than the flexible clad alternative.

A fine restored 168 with Sirocco flexible cab at a show and parked next to a 165 with the rigid Sankey cabin.

An original 185 at the Cheffins sale ground in Cambridgeshire. The 185 arrived in 1971 and replaced the earlier 178 model. Note the PAVT rear wheels and how complete this off-farm tractor is.

The cladding was extended around the sides of the engine to help direct heat into the cab itself during the winter months and worked very well according to my father, who used these tractors a lot in the 1970s! The 185 used the Perkins A4.248 to produce 75 hp.

The 188 was the 'luxury class' version of the 185 and shared the same engine. The doors have been removed from this example while ploughing, probably to let the heat and noise out!

A Four-Wheel Traction conversion of the 165 with the Selene drive system, the propshaft of which can be seen behind the front wheel.

even an equal size wheel version was offered for the 175 and 178. The firm also offered a turbocharger kit to boost the power of the Perkins A4.248 engine to 84.5 hp.

In America power requirements were increasing all the time and it was in 1970 that Massey Ferguson launched the giant articulated four-wheel-drive 1500 tractor with 150 hp available from a Caterpillar 3150 V8 engine, which was later joined by the even larger 180 hp 1800. The 1200 tractor made its appearance at the Smithfield Show in 1971 and was also an articulated four-wheel-drive machine, although this time with a more modest 105 hp rating from its Perkins A6.354 six-cylinder motor. Built in Britain at the MF Manchester factory that made industrial equipment, the 1200 was something very new to British farmers and was the first taste of articulated tractor power for many. Complete with integrated safety cab, which also met the later quiet cab legislation, the 1200 was built until 1980, when it was replaced by the more powerful 1250 model; still an articulated four-wheel-drive machine, but now with 112 hp from its Perkins A6.354.4 motor.

The 1100 led to a range of four high-horsepower rigid-frame tractors in the early 1970s, but only the largest two of these made their way over to Britain from 1975. The 1135 featured a six-cylinder Perkins AT6.354 turbocharged engine producing 135 hp, while the 1155 used a Perkins V8 AV8.540 diesel to provide 155 hp. The 1505 articulated model was also shown at the 1975 Smithfield Show with power coming from a V8 Caterpillar 3208 engine producing a heady 185 hp. The even more powerful 210 hp 1805 was also built for the North American market.

This Massey Ferguson 135 narrow tractor was used for orchard work in the south of England. Note how the Duncan cab fits over the original 'shell'-type rear wings.

Industrial versions of the 35 and 65 and the 100 Series were built at Manchester using skid units from Coventry. Note the square bonnet and Duncan safety cab fitted to this example, now used on a Sussex farm after its life in the construction industry has come to an end.

The Massey Ferguson 1200 looked unlike any other tractor that the British farmer was used to when it was launched at the Smithfield Show at the end of 1971. With equal size wheels, four-wheel-drive and articulated steering, this tractor was a very capable machine despite its modest 105 horses.

Big two-wheel-drive tractors were at the heart of the North American tractor industry where they were seen as high draft machines. A six-cylinder Perkins turbocharged diesel engine powered this 1135, seen in Lincolnshire.

The 1155 was the flagship of the big two-wheel-drive range of the 1970s getting its mighty 155 hp from a Perkins V8 engine. Looking enormous to most British farmers, a few of this and the 1135 model were sold in the UK from 1974.

A Caterpillar V8 engine, producing 185 hp, was the source of power in the 1505 articulated tractor. Articulated four-wheel-drive tractors were an important part of the North American tractor line for many years.

CHAPTER 3

Comfort First

The 1080 model built in France was a useful addition to the 100 Series range but it always seemed to have issues, mostly to do with the Perkins engine fitted. Unfortunately some of these problems were taken over to the new model that replaced it in 1974, despite the fact that this was a very new-looking design. However, the new 595, as it was called, still used the same Perkins A4.318 four-cylinder motor to produce 88 hp.

The 595 was very much an impressive looking machine, showing off as it did some very new features including a brand-new integrally designed cab that was designed as part of the new tractor, rather than just an add on. What is more it was a 'quiet cab', one of the first that met noise level legislation that would be introduced in 1976 in the UK. The 595 may have had its problems but it was still a very capable machine, it had power to spare and even in two-wheel-drive form it was an excellent tractor for heavy cultivation work and ploughing, helped by the fact, no doubt, that it was quite a bit heavier than the 188. The 595 was, in fact, to be the first in a complete new range of tractors designed to replace most of the 100 Series models two years later.

The full 500 range was duly launched in 1976 and was made up of the three-cylinder 550, four-cylinder 560, 565, 575 and 590 and the existing 595. All featured the same styling as the 595 with the square 'Supercab', as MF called the 'Q' cab, and square bonnet lines that were much less fussy than the earlier 100 Series machines and also included a 'hard nose' radiator surround at the front. The 500 range was a significant improvement on the old 100 Series, with the fuel tank now moved from its traditional position on top of the engine to down under the cab on the left-hand side, allowing better access to the top of the engine compartment, helped by a more easily removed bonnet design. Changeable output shafts on the new power take-off allowed 540 and 1,000 rpm operation plus synchromesh was now used on the eight-speed standard transmission.

The new 550 replaced the 148 with its 47 hp Perkins AD3.152S engine and was the only three-cylinder model in the 500 Series lineup. The smallest four-cylinder tractor was the 56 hp 560 with Perkins AD4.203 engine followed by the 60 hp 565 with Perkins A4.236 motor, both models replacing the 165, while the 575 was a 66 hp machine and replaced the 168, also using the Perkins A4.236 engine. The 590 became the new 185 and 188 with 75 hp on tap from its A4.248S Perkins engine. There was also an 85 hp 592 model

The 595 brought the first glimpse of a new range of Massey Ferguson tractor for the 1970s. Launched in 1974, the 595 used a four-cylinder Perkins engine of 88 hp and was built in Beauvais, France as the replacement for the 1080 model.

for certain markets as a slightly less powerful version of the 595, but not in the UK. The 592 and 595 were only built at Beauvais, but the smaller range was built in both Coventry and France, although specification often varied.

These new, well-appointed tractors were also offered with several optional extras as well as the choice between a basic eight-speed gearbox or the Multi-Power twelve-speed transmission, including independent and live power take-off.

From 1978 factory-fitted four-wheel-drive became an option on the 575 and 590, which was a good move given the rising popularity of this idea, but the power outputs proved to be rather limited to get the full potential out of this fitment, and many were given extra horses by fitting an Opico turbocharger to the engine as an aftermarket enhancement.

The 595 Mark II appeared in 1977 with a redesigned gearbox and more powerful hydraulic system. There were problems with the 500 Series though, and this led to many improvements being made as the years passed, including a two-door cab that was something demanded by many users who disliked the single door arrangement.

In 1981 the 600 Series arrived as a kind of 'Mark II 500 Series' with many improvements including a new cab. The 675 at 66 hp replaced the earlier 565 and 575 while the 75 hp 690 replaced the 590, and the 88 hp 698 replaced the 595.

The baby of the 500 range was the 550, using the trusty Perkins AD3.152S engine, which was the latest version of the engine first used in the 35X.

The 565 was a 60 hp tractor with a four-cylinder Perkins motor. The new Supercab was designed from the start as part of the tractor itself rather than just an add-on, but lacked an offside opening door as shown here, although the single-piece side window could be opened for ventilation.

Sat in a barn in Norfolk between jobs, this still-working 575 is a superb example of the breed and was a good all-rounder of a tractor thanks to its lively 66 hp engine. The Supercab was painted red on the lower half and grey on the upper portion and roof on the original 500 Series tractors, as can be seen clearly here.

The 590 had 75 hp available under its new-look square bonnet. The use of the big MF decal on the bonnet sides followed its first appearance on the 1200 model.

This 590 is also fitted with a powered front axle and is shown on display at the Grassland '96 demonstration in Warwickshire. These tractors were often fitted with Opico turbochargers to increase the standard 75 horses into more like 85 hp. Note the all-red cab fitted to later build tractors towards the end of 500 Series production.

In 1977 the 595 Mark II arrived with a number of improvements. This example has been fitted with an Opico turbocharger to boost the power from its Perkins A4.318 from 88 hp to nearly 100 hp.

This late 590 was actually sold to its original owner after the new 600 Series had arrived and is fitted with the all-red cab. It is shown collecting oats from a Massey Ferguson 525 combine in East Sussex.

The interior of the Supercab was functional with everything the driver needed easily to hand. The dashboard has evolved considerably from the 100 Series but the two gear levers are still positioned centrally on the floor.

The new cab was lighter and gave better visibility, plus it came with two-doors! A square style bonnet was retained with the 'hard nose' radiator surround and these proved to be very durable and worthy successors to the earlier machines and came with the option of either twelve forward and four reverse synchromesh transmission or the Multi-Power version.

A six-cylinder, range topping model was added in 1984 when the 98 hp 699 arrived along with a new 698T model that featured a turbocharger to produce 90 hp and replaced the earlier 698. These were very impressive machines that addressed many aspects that farmers had asked for and were, like the rest of the 600 Series, available with the option of four-wheel-drive. The 699 featured a very smooth running and powerful Perkins A6.354.4 six pot motor mated to the twelve-speed gearbox.

The 698T turned the earlier 698 tractor into a real 'pocket rocket', with a much livelier performance with more power, yet still in a compact package.

The new cab and revised styling hid the fact that the 600 Series, launched in 1981, was basically a re-worked 500 Series design. The 675 was the smallest with a Perkins A4.236 engine producing 66 hp. This example is planting sugar beet in Suffolk.

The 690 was powered by the Perkins A4.248S engine rated at 75 hp. The Italian-sourced cabs were prone to corrosion at even a fairly young age but this example looks in very good condition.

The 698T arrived in 1984 as a replacement for the original 698 model, more power being squeezed from its Perkins four-cylinder engine by the fitting of a turbocharger from new, hence the 'T' designation in the model number.

From 1984 the flagship of the 600 Series was the 699 with a Perkins six-cylinder engine of 100 hp providing the motive force. Two-wheel-drive versions were still quite common at this stage and the new design of the 600 range saw the triple triangle MF badge disappear from the front of the radiator in favour of a new square alternative with just the MF lettering.

CHAPTER 4

True Powerhouses

In 1979 the Beauvais factory began production of a new 2000 Series of tractors – machines that would be the largest Massey Ferguson tractors to be built in Europe so far. Slightly earlier, a range of very large 2000 Series tractors were introduced to North American farmers, replacing the range that had been topped by the 1135 and 1155 tractors. However, the French-built 2000 range only really had the transmissions, cab and tinwork in common with these monster machines. The cab was certainly new and extremely spacious with previously unheard of areas of glass, giving superb all-round visibility from the tractor seat and accessed through a single door. The new transmission was called Speedshift and gave a shuttle reverse function plus sixteen forward and twelve reverse modes that were controlled by small levers mounted up to the right of the suspended driving seat.

Smallest of the new range initially was the 110 hp 2640, which was joined by the bigger 126 hp 2680. These two models led the charge followed by the 93 hp 2620 and 147 hp 2720 models in 1981. All four were powered by Perkins six-cylinder A6.3544 engines, with the 2680 and 2720 being turbocharged to get the extra horses, and with all of them being available in two- or four-wheel-drive form.

Rear-mounted fuel tanks, powerful hydraulic linkage and power to spare made the 2000 Series tractors ideal for heavy cultivation work, the Perkins smooth six-cylinder engines being able to deliver plenty of torque and lugging ability. The baby 2620 always seemed a bit underpowered for its size though, and was effectively replaced by the 699 model in 1984.

Larger tractors had also appeared in North America in the form of a whole range of articulated powerhouses. First offered for sale in the UK in 1980, the 4000 Series models were important as they were the first Massey Ferguson tractors to be fitted with an electronically controlled hydraulic linkage system – a real taste of things to come in the future. Launched in the States in 1978, the range was made up of three models, with eighteen-speed transmissions, stretching from 225 hp up to 320 hp; the middle 260 hp 4840 model, powered by a Cummins V8 diesel engine, was the tractor offered in Britain from 1980.

The 2005 range of six-cylinder tractors replaced the 2000 line built in France in 1985 with the only real change being the electronically controlled rear linkage, hence the 'Electronic' name proudly displayed in red on the bonnets of these tractors. A two-door cab was also a new feature and the range stretched from the 110 hp 2645 up to the 147 hp 2725, with the 130 hp 2685 sitting in the middle.

The French-built 2000 range arrived in 1979 with all four models arriving by 1981 and all featuring Perkins six-cylinder A6.3544 engines, the 2640 being fuelled to produce 110 hp. This is a later example with the square MF badge on the front radiator grille instead of the triple triangle badge used at the beginning of 2000 Series production.

A fully restored example of the 126 hp 2680, which used a turbocharged version of the Perkins six-cylinder engine. The size of the cab is clearly evident on these tractors, as is the single huge one-piece door.

Inside the cab of the 2000 Series the controls were unlike any other tractor, with the sixteen forward and twelve reverse Speedshift transmission being controlled by these levers up beside the seat.

The 2620 was the smallest in the range at 93 hp and also the shortest lived, only being produced from 1981 to 1984. In many ways it was quite a heavy machine for its fairly modest power rating and this example is seen in an auction lineup.

With 260 hp available from its 260 hp Cummins V8 motor, the 4840 was the largest MF model to be offered in Britain for several years. This example is shown tucked away in the back of a barn in Norfolk.

In 1985 the 2005 Series arrived with the 2645 now the smallest in the range with its 110 hp. The large cab had been reworked to provide two doors and new decals added to emphasise the fitting of electronically controlled rear linkage.

The word 'electronic' in red stylised font was added to the bonnet decals to show that these tractors were a step up from what had gone before.

The 147 hp 2725 was the flagship model in the 2005 range and also the largest tractor to be built at the Beauvais factory in France so far.

CHAPTER 5

Tractors for the World

This ever-increasing size and sophistication was all well and good, but not every farmer in the world wanted big machines with electronic controls. The 100 Series, originally known as the Red Giants, may have been left in the shade by all the bigger tractors and new developments, but they had been extremely successful tractors for Massey Ferguson, their reliability and ease of use being big plus points not only in less developed parts of the world but also in the UK for certain tasks. The 135 was a very popular little machine and remained in production long after the other original models had disappeared, the last versions surviving up to the end of the 1970s with a quick detach cab.

In 1979 the first new models designed to finally replace the 135 appeared when the 45 hp 240 and 60 hp 265 arrived. The 265 effectively replaced the 565 model, which was soon to be phased out, and these fairly basic tractors had the eight-speed transmission and a very wide range of cab options provided by various outside firms. There were options also available to the purchaser, such as Multi-Power and power steering, but the idea was to offer a no-frills machine. As the 1980s began to unfold further models joined the 200 Series lineup, all made in the factory at Coventry, including the 33 hp 230, 75 hp 290, 47 hp 250, 66 hp 275 and 88 hp 298.

Most of the 200 Series was replaced by the new and improved 300 Series tractors in 1986, leaving only the little 230 and 240 models and some variants, to keep the earlier range alive. Although still produced at Coventry as basic specification machines, the new 300 tractors had a lot more options than previously, with the larger tractors having as much as five different gearbox configurations available. Four-wheel-drive was also an option on the larger tractors and the 399 flagship of the range was the first six-cylinder tractor to be built at Banner Lane.

With models from 47 to 97 hp, the 300 Series was pretty comprehensive and various new models were added later, such as the 58 hp 360 and the 90 hp turbocharged 390T. The original cabs were updated for 1988 when a choice of either a Low Profile or Hi-Line flat-floor cab, with side-mounted gear levers in the top-spec version. The 399 eventually pumped out 104 hp thanks to a new Perkins six-cylinder motor in the early 1990s, a year that also saw the new 59 hp 362 appear. The 300 Series all but disappeared in 1997 when new models were introduced, although some of the smaller models did remain in production for a time.

The 265 was one of the two original models introduced in 1979 that, at 60 hp, was an alternative to the 565 at the time.

A different 265 is shown while picking up round hay bales with a Farmhand front loader, and shows how the cabs fitted differed widely even on the same model of tractor. Power for the 265 came from a four-cylinder Perkins A4.236 engine.

The little 230 was quite a late addition to the range and was really an economy version of the popular 240 model with 33 hp available from its Perkins three-cylinder engine.

Looking a little tired at a Cheffins auction, the 66 hp 275 was a later addition with a little more power than the 265 tractor. Factory-fitted four-wheel-drive was now becoming a much more popular choice for farmers in Britain.

This 290 still earns its keep on a farm in the East Midlands and is shown consolidating a seedbed with a set of Cambridge rolls. Fitted with the top of the range Duncan Supercab in this instance, the 290 was powered by a Perkins four-cylinder A4.248S engine of 75 hp.

88 hp was on offer from the 298, which made it equal to the 595 and the 698 tractors, but despite sharing the 500 Series styling, the 298 did not look as large as the 595 tractor.

This 265 and 290 look superb at auction and show how the export market 200 Series tractors were sold. They share the pre-cleaner bowls fitted on tractors destined for dustier climates than the UK.

The little 240 was a very capable machine with its Perkins AD3.152 engine providing 45 hp, this tractor being used for ploughing matches, complete with a very spacious looking Duncan cab.

Largest of the 300 Series models launched in 1986 was the 399, the only tractor in the range to feature a six-cylinder Perkins engine – in this case the A6.354 unit. Note the black cab with red roof that was fitted to the early 300 Series tractors.

Another early member of the family, the 350 replaced the 250 with more power available from its Perkins AD3.152 engine with a rating of 52 hp.

In 1988 new cabs arrived, now painted in all-over grey. The 390 had been popular from the beginning among both livestock and arable farmers with its four-cylinder 81 hp engine proving a lively performer, if perhaps somewhat underpowered for some tasks, the power coming from a Perkins A4.248 unit.

Another 390 in the south of England, this time on a task that the 300 Series was designed for in many respects, feeding cattle within the confines of farm buildings.

The little 362 tractor with its Perkins four-cylinder A4.236 engine providing 62 hp was a powerful machine in a small package. The highways version was the 362H, but this one has been returned to agriculture for use in ploughing matches.

The last versions of the 399 benefitted from more power thanks to a Perkins Quadram six-cylinder engine of 104 hp, making this model even more desirable, not only at the time, but also on the second-hand market today.

CHAPTER 6

Tractors for the Future

The year 1986 was a landmark one, not only for Massey Ferguson but also for the history of tractors! That's a big statement to live up to, but when Massey Ferguson launched the 3000 Series tractors in that year it would prove be the beginning of the modern tractor as we know it today.

Exhaustive testing was carried out with prototype machines to make sure that the main principles of these new tractors would work in real farm situations – a necessary precaution given the game changing attributes of what would become the 3000 Series.

The big launch in 1986 saw the public get their first look at this range of tractors, which spanned from the four-cylinder 68 hp 3050, up to the six-cylinder 109 hp 3090. A square bonnet was retained but with better access made possible through removable side panels, while the new cab was designed with driver ergonomics firmly in mind, and had two wide opening doors and a three-piece rear windscreen with the two thick pillars supporting the doors being the widest used, giving extremely good forwards visibility extending to around the sides.

Two tall gear levers positioned to the right of the driving seat controlled the gearbox on these tractors together with the Speedshift buttons mounted on a console to the right of the driver, giving either sixteen or thirty-two speeds depending on the specification chosen. This console was also used to hold the controls for the hydraulic system, which was a very simple to use panel with knobs and switches giving full, and fingertip, control of the rear hydraulics. But that wasn't all, Massey Ferguson called the 3000 the 'thinking tractors' and the reason for this was the amount of automatic functions controlled by the Autotronic system which could engage and disengage the diff-lock and power take-off as well as four-wheel-drive when braking, just some of the clever features designed to take the load off the driver and also to protect the tractors systems.

Autotronic was the entry-level version. If you wanted even more futuristic controls then the purchaser could opt for the Datatronic version which used a computer interface, mounted on the right-hand side wide pillar, to control such options as wheelslip percentages and other aspects of the tractors performance, including pre-programming to get the best performance from the tractor in whatever conditions were being encountered.

Four-cylinder engines were used on the 3050, 3060 and 3070 models while the 3080 and 3090 were six-cylinder tractors, all using Perkins power plants as would be expected.

The 3000 Series introduced in 1986 ushered in a new era of tractor technology. The 3070 was the largest four-cylinder tractor in the range with 93 hp on tap from a Perkins AT4.236 turbocharged engine, making it quite a powerful tractor in a compact package. With new tinwork and new cabs the 3000 Series looked unlike any other tractor before and this example is also a top-specification Datatronic version, with full electronic function management.

The 3080 was the smallest six-cylinder model in the new range and also perhaps the best selling, its Perkins A6.354.4 engine pumping out 100 hp. The 3000 Series were usually fitted with straight, narrow exhaust pipes, the silencer being placed under the bonnet to provide better visibility. This 3080 ploughing in East Sussex is an entry-level Autotronic version, but still with much more sophistication than any of its competitors when it was new.

The largest model in the 3000 Series was originally the 3090 with 109 hp from its six-cylinder Perkins A6.3544 engine. With the choice of either sixteen or thirty-two-speed synchromesh transmissions, in addition to the electronic hydraulics and other functions, the 3090 and its sisters were well ahead of their time.

The following year the big, six-cylinder 3600 Series arrived, built like the smaller 3000 Series in Beauvais. Replacing the 2005 range, the new 113 hp 3610, 133 hp 3630 and 150 hp 3650 brought the Autotronic and Datatronic features up the power scale and shared the same cab and styling as their smaller siblings. A sixteen-speed transmission was fitted, complete with a forward and reverse shuttle and Speedshift button controlled splitter.

The 3600 range was revamped for the 1990s with the 142 hp 3645 and 155 hp 3655 replacing the earlier models and joined by a new flagship; the 180 hp 3680. This big machine was now the largest built so far at Beauvais but was different to any others in the range, not only in that it had a pronounced slope to the end of the longer bonnet, but also by the fact that a Valmet engine lurked under that bonnet, instead of a Perkins unit. The 3680 was not produced for long before it was replaced by the 170 hp 3670 and 190 hp 3690, both powered by Valmet engines built in Finland. In a reciprocal agreement Valmet sold these large Massey Ferguson tractors in their own colours on their home market to top out the firms own range. This working relationship with Valmet, later Valtra, would be an enduring one.

The early 1990s saw many improvements to the 'thinking tractors', including the 3065 model that was also available in a high-visibility version with a steeply sloping bonnet. Another new model had been introduced previously called the 3115, which fitted in the gap between the 3000 and 3600 ranges and this was joined by the bigger 3125 and then in 1992 by the 3120, which replaced the 3115. The 3120, powered by a new Perkins Quadram six-cylinder engine, was designed to be a lighter tractor than the 3125. A 3635 model of 132 hp was also added as was a brand-new semi-powershift option called Dynashift.

1987 saw the benefits of the 3000 Series taken further up the power scale with the advent of the 3600 Series replacing the 2005 models. The 3630 was the middle machine in the original range with 133 hp on tap from its Perkins six-cylinder motor.

This well cared for 3645 from Norfolk represents the second generation of 3600 Series tractors, this being the smallest in the range initially with 142 hp on tap from its Perkins 1006.T six-cylinder turbocharged engine. Note the large front linkage, replacement exhaust pipe and unusual bonnet decal on this specimen!

The 3655 replaced the 3650 with its Perkins six-cylinder 1006.TWG motor providing 155 horses. Although it has clocked up over 10,000 hours working for a Norfolk contractor, this 3655 is still in stunning condition and is also fitted with the Dynashift semi-powershift transmission introduced in the early 1990s.

The 3690 also used the Valmet engine but tweaked to provide 190 hp. The thirty-two-speed transmission was also now fitted to the 3600 Series instead of the earlier sixteen-speed version.

The 3680 was the new flagship model and it certainly looked it with its longer bonnet complete with distinctive slope at the front. Under that bonnet resided a Valmet 612DS six-cylinder turbocharged engine of 180 hp. The 3680 was the first MF model built in Beauvais to move away from Perkins power since 1959.

The 3065 was the first new addition to the original 3000 lineup and was also produced as a high-visibility model with a steeply sloping bonnet. This Suffolk example, complete with Stoll front loader, is of the conventional type and is powered by a Perkins four-cylinder AC4.236 engine of 85 hp.

The 3115 model bridged the gap between the largest 3000 model and the smallest 3600 series tractor with a Perkins 1006 six-cylinder engine providing 115 hp. Later models in all the MF ranges had the front badge, which had reverted to a new version of the triple triangle of old, mounted centrally on the radiator grille rather than to the top left as previously.

The Datatronic interface, mounted on the inside of the right-hand cab pillar, was controlled by a single knob, with information displayed on the small LED screen at the top. The list of functions clearly shows how advanced these tractors actually were.

The 3125 further bridged the gap between the two ranges and was a heavier version of the 3115 with 126 hp available from a Perkins six-cylinder 1006.T turbocharged engine.

The 3085 was an improved version of the 3080 still with 100 hp, but now from a six-cylinder Perkins 1006 engine, and the Dynashift semi-powershift was now also an option. This very high-houred example seen while topping potatoes in Suffolk is fitted with the standard Speedshift transmission, which still gave thirty-two gears in both forward and reverse but without the powershift steps.

Dynashift combined the existing gearbox with a four-range powershift that could be selected without using the clutch and was controlled by a small lever up on the left of the steering column which, along with the two tall gear levers, controlled the thirty-two forward and thirty-two reverse speeds. At a time when most manufacturers were beginning to fit their larger tractors with full powershift transmissions, the Dynashift was seen by MF as a cheaper alternative that gave the same benefits as a full powershift but without the substantial extra sophistication. And, indeed, Dynashift was an excellent and very reliable system, giving superb control of a broad range of gears for every task, plus it gave an auto-changing feature at high speed on the road.

The very last of the 3000 Series models to be introduced was the 3075, which appeared in 1993 based on the 93 hp 3070 model, but was now fitted with the option of Dynashift. Previously the 3085, which had earlier replaced the 3080, had been the smallest offered with this transmission. The 3075 featured a four-cylinder turbocharged Perkins engine producing 98 hp, making it a powerful tractor in a small package.

Meanwhile the farm machinery business in general was once again in the doldrums and there were many mergers and takeovers in the 1980s. In 1989 Massey Ferguson sold its interest in Landini, an Italian firm that was producing many tractors from the Massey Ferguson stable in their own colours and with minor alterations, but at the same time was providing wheeled and crawler tractors to sell in MF livery. Massey Ferguson had took control of Landini back in 1959 and so it was in the MF fold for thirty years when it was sold to ARGO, an Italian family-owned business, in 1989.

The transmission in the 3085 was still controlled by the two tall gear levers – the one to the right being a forward and reverse shuttle, the other lever controlling the rest of the gears thanks to a sideward shift feature.

Massey Ferguson managed to ride out the difficult 1980s with various management changes. A new holding company called Varity Corporation was created but in 1994 the agricultural division was sold off to AGCO and with that a new era would begin.

Last of the line, the 3075 was a more powerful version of the 3070 with 98 hp available from its four-cylinder turbocharged Perkins engine. This proved to be a very popular model during its fairly brief production life and certainly lived up to its reputation as a powerful 'pocket rocket'!

The 3635 boasted a Perkins six-cylinder 1006T turbocharged engine of 132 hp giving a heavier tractor for this power bracket once again after the demise of the original 3630. The 3635 might have been a heavier tractor but it was still versatile enough for work such as de-stoning potato beds. Fitted with the excellent Dynashift transmission, it was a joy to use on such work as well.

CHAPTER 7

New Owners

AGCO was an acronym for Allis-Gleaner Corporation, which had only been formed in 1990, based in Georgia in the USA. Although a young company, the firm actually had its roots firmly in established farm machinery companies and was formed after the German KFD company (trading as Deutz-Allis after earlier purchasing the Allis-Chalmers business) decided to pull out of North America. The firm's American management bought the firm and turned it into AGCO, selling the Allis-Gleaner, Hesston and White brands. Massey Ferguson now joined this portfolio of agricultural businesses and later more would join it.

The first signs of change under the new ownership was the launch of two new ranges to replace the existing 3000, 3100 and 3600 tractors, which were, by now, needing something of a makeover to keep them competitive. The result was the 80 to 190 hp 6100 and 8100 Series that built on the existing models features but came with a new cab with greater glass area and a new version of the Autotronic and Datatronic tractor management systems, while the Dynashift transmission was now offered on all models. Still built in France, the flagship of the range was the impressive 200 hp 8160, now the largest tractor to be built at Beauvais but later to be usurped by the mighty 8180 in 1998, with 260 hp available from its Valmet six-cylinder engine, which was turbocharged and intercooled. An eighteen-speed full powershift transmission was also included in the specification on the largest model instead of the Dynashift semi-powershift, and all the 8100 Series, and the six-cylinder 6100 models, benefitted from a side-mounted exhaust stack instead of the traditional bonnet-mounted pipe.

Later the 6190 arrived, fitting in at the top end of this series with a Perkins six-cylinder engine producing 130 hp and providing a lighter alternative to the 8110 model.

In 1995 the result of badge engineering within AGCO saw the introduction of a large tractor badged as the Massey Ferguson 9240, which was actually a White tractor from the AGCO stable painted in MF colours. A six-cylinder 240 hp Cummins turbocharged engine supplied the power driving through a full powershift eighteen forward by nine reverse transmission. Only a few were sold in the UK as this was really an American specification machine and did not appeal to many farmers this side of the Atlantic.

It was in 1997 that a new 4200 range, built at Coventry, largely replaced the 300 Series. The 52 to 110 hp 4200 range offered no fewer than three different versions of cab and also some automated features, although the 300 Series principles of basic tractor control was retained.

The new order and shape out in force at the 1996 Grassland demonstration with 6180, 8130 and 8160 models on display. New cabs, bonnets and features plus side-mounted exhausts across the six-cylinder tractors meant that these were certainly new-looking machines when launched in 1995.

The 6150 replaced the 3075 as the new pocket rocket four-cylinder model in the range with its Perkins turbocharged 1004.4 engine putting out 98 hp.

This 6170 is based on a Suffolk dairy farm where it is the main prime mover with 110 hp from a six-cylinder Perkins 1006.6 engine. The Dynashift semi-powershift transmission was now available throughout the range and this view clearly shows the new side-mounted exhaust stack that was fitted to all six-cylinder models in both the 6100 and bigger 8100 tractors.

The 120 hp 6180 replaced the 3120 and was a 120 hp tractor, and the largest in the 6100 range, when it was introduced.

The smallest of the 8100 range is shown here spreading slurry in Sussex. With a Perkins six-cylinder engine of 135 hp the 8110 is no meek performer and can handle heavy trailers and tankers, as well as heavy cultivations. This contractors' machine is also fitted with a front linkage which, although an aftermarket fitment, would soon become a more common factory-fitted option.

This Massey Ferguson 8130 is at work in Suffolk with a Lely power harrow and has 155 hp under its bonnet as the replacement for the 3655.

When the 8100 Series arrived in 1995, the 200 hp 8160 was the largest tractor built at Beauvais in France. Like the 3670, 3680 and 3690 before it, the 8160 was powered by a Valmet engine made in Finland; in the case of the 8160, this was a six-cylinder turbocharged 634DS unit.

The Massey Ferguson 9240 is actually an American-built White tractor in disguise. Imported into the European market to top out the 8100 range, the 9240 had 240 hp available from a turbocharged and intercooled six-cylinder Cummins engine. Its dramatic appearance belied its American parentage but the back axle was actually made in Britain, by David Brown no less!

A steeply sloping bonnet is the order of the day for this 4245 tractor, built in Coventry and shown planting potatoes in East Sussex. Launched in 1997, the 4200 Series was made up of both sloping and standard bonnet tractors and were fitted with a lower profile version of the cab fitted to the larger MF tractors. A Perkins 1004.4TW four-cylinder engine provided 85 hp under that droop nose.

In 2001 the 6100 and 8100 Series tractors were replaced by the improved 6200 and 8200 models, which addressed a few issues that were encountered on some of the earlier tractors. Only the 85 hp 6245 and 95 hp 6255 had four-cylinder engines, the rest of the 6200 and 8200 lineup using six-cylinder Perkins or Valtra engines. New options on these tractors included a front axle suspension system, automatic gear changes and a more sophisticated management system, as well as a new look with all-red bonnets and decals. The highly regarded Dynashift thirty-two-speed transmission was still a feature as was the Datatronic II terminal, still mounted to the cab pillar but now re-designed with more functions available. A new feature on the 8200 models was the PowerControl system, which used a lever on the driving-seat armrest in conjunction with a paddle under the steering wheel to the left.

The 8200 models later received a facelift with the introduction of the Xtra range with enhanced specification and features to keep them competitive, the Xtra name being proudly displayed on the sides of the bonnet.

With the introduction of the 6200 range in 2001, models such as the 6255 were still available with the sloping bonnet option. A Perkins turbocharged four-cylinder Perkins engine provided the 95 hp that is enabling this Sussex tractor to bale straw and also pick the bales up afterwards with its Quicke front loader.

This 6270, collecting grass from a forage harvester powered by an 8220 tractor, shows how the 6200 Series was very similar to the 6100 range, but the new colour scheme and new bonnets helped them stand out well. In the cab was where the most new features came into play, with new controls and the Datatronic II system.

The 'Power Control' decal on the bonnet shows this 6290 is fitted with the paddle for gear selection through the Dynashift transmission.

The 8200 range also arrived in 2001 with the same slightly rejigged appearance as the 6200 tractors. This well-worked 150 hp East Sussex 8220 is shown in the midst of flying grass as it collects the crop in a trailer.

The 8240 had 160 hp on tap from its Sisu six-cylinder engine. Sisu were the parent company of Valmet who changed the engine building concerns name and also that of the tractors they produced, first to Valtra Valmet and then just Valtra.

Taking a break from powering a Pottinger forage harvester, this 8220 Xtra is in fine fettle and was the largest tractor used by an East Sussex-based contractor for many years.

With 160 hp on tap from its Perkins engine, the 8220 Xtra was equally at home with a five-furrow plough or on carting duties. A full set of wafer weights is needed on the front of the tractor to provide front-end ballast to counteract the heavy plough.

Inside the cab of the 8220 Xtra the main controls are positioned on the seat armrest and to the right on the console over the rear wheel. Everything comes easily to hand and the other gear controls are positioned on a paddle under the steering wheel to the left-hand side.

The Datatronic II terminal – in this case seen inside the cab of the 8220 Xtra – was still positioned on the right-hand side cab pillar but now featured a much larger screen.

CHAPTER 8

All Change

For decades the Beauvais factory in France and the Banner Lane plant in Coventry in the UK had worked more or less side by side, but with the introduction of the 3000 Series in 1986 it became evident that Coventry was now only to build the lower specification tractors, such as the then-new 300 Series. This, perhaps inevitably, led to the eventual closure of the Banner Lane factory in 2002, bringing to an end production of Massey Ferguson tractors in Britain; the smaller tractor ranges now being produced either in Beauvais, or by using badge-engineered machines brought in from Valtra.

The new 4400 range was built in Finland using the existing Valtra A Series as a platform, but the 5400 Series was a development of the 4300 range, which replaced the 4200 Series originally built in Coventry and provided more of a cross-over, technology-wise, from the two ranges. In fact, the 5400 range has ended up with some pretty sophisticated four-cylinder models that many farmers use as prime movers as an alternative to the larger models.

AGCO meanwhile had continued its spending spree, bringing the German-built Fendt tractors into the fold in 1997, the Challenger brand from Caterpillar in 2002, and Valtra in 2004. All these acquisitions would end up having a large impact on the Massey Ferguson brand.

The Fendt connection was the first to be seen when the new Massey Ferguson 6400 and 7400 ranges were launched in 2003 to replace the 6200 and some of the 8200 machines. The 6400 used an updated version of the semi-powershift Dynashift transmission known as Dyna 6, with six speeds in each range instead of four. Originally only six-cylinder models were offered but these were soon joined by four-cylinder variants.

The 120–185 hp 7400 range was fitted with a version of the Fendt Vario stepless, or constantly variable, transmission called Dyna-VT. Pioneered by Fendt in the 1990s, the Vario transmission basically meant that there were no gears as such, giving seamless speed changes and the ability to just drive the tractor using the hand or foot throttle with the tractor doing the rest. Needless to say, the specification of these tractors was very high and both the 6400 and 7400 ranges benefitted from the very latest versions of the Datatronic computer monitoring and automatic control of nearly all functions.

These were followed in 2004 by the update of the larger 8200 models into the 8400 range of tractors from 215 to 290 hp, complete with the Dyna-VT transmission and making the new flagship 8480 the biggest Beauvais-built tractor so far. The new computer controlled

The 100 hp Massey Ferguson 4455 is actually a re-badged Valtra A Series tractor and was built in Finland.

The 5400 range are built in Beauvais and this 5455 is shown rolling a seedbed in Suffolk. A Perkins four-cylinder 1104 turbocharged engine provides 95 hp and a 16 ratio Speedshift transmission is fitted as standard, with this example being equipped with Dyna-4, similar to the original Dynashift.

This 5460 is using a power harrow to make a tilth for sugar beet in Suffolk. The 5460 was a 105 hp tractor but still fitted with a Perkins 1104 turbocharged four-cylinder motor.

Even more power was on offer from the 5470 model thanks to a Sisu 44DT engine producing 125 hp. Four cylinders were still the order of the day though, as the fashion for higher power four pot tractors grew. This 5470 is taking a break from silage carting in East Sussex.

Busy carting grain from the combine, this 6495 complete with Dynashift transmission shows off the new 6400 lines well. Representing the ever-increasing use of Sisu engines, the 6495 is powered by a six-cylinder and intercooled unit.

Above: This 6499 was brand-new when pictured in 2005, was the largest tractor in the 6400 lineup and is also equipped with a factory fitted front linkage.

Left: A look through the wide opening door into the cab of the 6499 shows clearly how much the interior had evolved over the years, with a flat floor, armrest seat controls and all the operating controls mounted on the binnacle to the right of the driver.

A Massey Ferguson 6480, brand spanking new and complete with chafer trailed sprayer, on demonstration from dealers Crawfords in Essex.

The Dyna-6 was a six-step semi-powershift transmission developed from the Dynashift gearbox and the type often chosen for the 6490. 170 hp was available from the 6490's Sisu 66CTA turbocharged six-cylinder motor.

The 7400 Series was similar to the larger 6400 models but featured the first glimpse of Fendt technology in a Massey Ferguson tractor as the constantly variable Dyna-VT transmission used in these tractors was derived from the Fendt Vario. This brand-new 7480 is equipped with a factory-fitted front linkage.

2004 saw the 8400 range replace the 8200 models and once again the styling was similar to the smaller tractor ranges, although there was certainly nothing small about these massive tractors! With 245 hp from its Sisu turbocharged and intercooled six-cylinder diesel engine, this 8460 has power to spare, planting oilseed rape straight into wheat stubble in Suffolk with a Sumo Trio.

The biggest of the 8400 range and now the largest Beauvais-built tractor so far was the 315 hp 8480, once again powered by a Sisu six-cylinder turbocharged and intercooled motor.

engine boost feature of the six-cylinder Sisu engines meant that these figures actually jumped to 235 and 315 hp, although this was only for transport and PTO work.

Various models in the 6400, 7400 and 8400 ranges were sold into the North American and Australian markets in Challenger colours and branding, and wider use was made across the range of Valtra engines, which were now known as Sisu Power engines. With the acquisition of Valtra and Sisu in 2004, AGCO got its own engine building facility and gradually AGCO Power engines would be used in its various brands.

There would also be more common usage of components between the various European arms of AGCO, but the Valtra, MF and Fendt brands would still maintain a very independent identity at the same time.

CHAPTER 9

Sixty Years On

From 2012 a new AGCO factory in Jackson, Minnesota began production of the larger Massey Ferguson models, which were also sold in Challenger colours, and saw the first production of American Massey Ferguson tractors since the late 1990s.

Continuous updates of the various ranges has led, from the early 2000s lineup of 2400, 3400, 5400, 6400, 7400 and 8400 tractors, to an even more concise range offered today. Various compact models from 19.5 to 46 hp make up the beginning of the current Massey Ferguson offering, followed by the various versions of 3600 models from 76 to 102 hp and including narrow and specialist versions for various applications.

The 4700 Series feature three-cylinder 3.3 litre AGCO Power engines and Dyna Synchroshift twelve-speed transmissions, while the 5600 range encompasses three- and four-cylinder 85 to 130 hp AGCO Power engines with a choice of either Dyna 4 or 6 transmissions, including models that take the three-cylinder engine over the 100 hp barrier for the first time. The 5700 lineup spans 100 to 110 hp and is powered by AGCO four-cylinder engines driving through a twelve-speed transmission and is joined by further 5700 SL models from 100–130 hp, with the choice of either Dyna 4 or Dyna 6 transmissions.

Going further up the power scale, the 6600 range encompasses models from 120 to 185 hp, all powered by four-cylinder AGCO Power engines while the similar 6700 range is made up of 120–130 hp models with four-cylinder engines and synchronised twelve-speed transmission. The 6700 S range is made up of 120–200 hp machines taking the four-cylinder engine up to a whopping 200 hp – a first for an agricultural tractor – and offered with either Dyna 4, Dyna 6 or Dyna VT transmission options. The 7700 range, on the other hand, offers the same transmission options but in six-cylinder tractors from 140 to 280 hp, and all use the AGCO SE3 Selective Catalytic Reduction system to reduce exhaust gas emissions.

The really large machines are the 8700 range, replacing the 8600 models, which saw brand-new cabs, and is made up of models from 270 to an earthshattering 400 hp from AGCO six-cylinder power units – the largest of which are the most powerful rigid-frame Massey Ferguson tractors ever built.

Built in Italy, the 3645 uses a 91 hp three-cylinder turbocharged and intercooled Sisu diesel and is part of the compact 3600 range, since replaced by newer models with the AGCO Power engines. This 3645 is a standard track model shown turning hay in Essex with a Krone rake.

The 4707 is the smallest in a range of three models that provide a return to basic tractors of the sort not seen since the demise of the 300 Series. An AGCO Power three-cylinder engine provides 75 hp and drives through a mechanical twelve-speed transmission.

The 5600 Series saw a higher level of sophistication come to this power class with a mixture of three- and four-cylinder AGCO Power engines providing the motive power. The 5610 model saw three-cylinder tractors cross the 100 hp barrier with a 105 hp rating while bigger four-cylinder models, such as this 120 hp 5612, could also be had with the steeply sloping bonnet option.

The 7600 Series replaced the 7400 range in 2013 with a further enhanced specification thanks to the use of the Fendt-designed computer monitoring systems and function control. This 7619 is using the power from its 170 hp AGCO Power engine to pull an Amazone drill at a dealer demonstration organized by Crawfords in Essex.

Biggest in the new range was the 7624, shown here with a Krone Big Pack square baler and with a maximum power output of 220 hp.

A view of the Fendt-derived Datatronic III terminal inside the cab of the 7624.

The 7600 Series had a pretty short lifespan before they were replaced by the 7700 range, with nine models available all powered by AGCO Power six-cylinder engines. The largest seven models have the choice of either Dyna-6 or Dyna-VT transmissions and the 7726 is the largest with a maximum power rating of 280 hp.

Shown on demonstration in Essex with front- and back-mounted Krone mower conditioners, the 8670 had a maximum output of 290 hp from its AGCO Power 84CTA turbocharged and intercooled engine.

Biggest of the lot is the 340 hp 8690 – a true powerhouse of a tractor built for the heaviest of farming tasks. It shares components with both Valtra and Fendt and is also sold in Challenger colours, representing the AGCO family of today.

CHAPTER 10

Legacy

Today AGCO keeps the spirit of Massey Ferguson very much alive and, despite being part of a large conglomerate, the MF name is still very well respected. The great numbers of enthusiasts who have preserved and restored the earlier tractors, as well as farmers who still use Massey Ferguson machines regularly that were new in the 1950s, all help keep the earlier glory days alive.

During its history MF has had a truly global influence on the world tractor market and has had many connections worldwide, including once owning the Ebro company from Spain,

A Massey Ferguson 3065 from the early 1990s comes together with a Massey Ferguson 35 from the early 1960s on a Suffolk farm. Both are still used regularly as part of the farming business.

the German Eicher concern and Landini. It has also entered into many manufacturing licenses with other companies, including IMT in the former Yugoslavia, Ursus in Poland, Tafe in India, AEIG in Iran and Farmwell in Sri Lanka – many of these firms building new versions of the old MF models, such as the 35 and 200 and 500 Series tractors.

As far as the vintage movement goes there are many enthusiasts of the MF brand and its earlier constituent companies, and in Britain there are the Friends of Ferguson Heritage and the Ferguson Club that keep the flag flying for a brand that was probably more responsible for shaping the modern tractor as we know it today than any other. Many restored tractors from the MF line can be seen at tractor shows or at rallies, showing what high regard the marque is still held.

The Massey Ferguson name also still graces combine harvesters and balers and under AGCO ownership this has spread once again into hay and forage equipment as well as material handlers. Under the auspices of AGCO, it looks as though the Massey Ferguson brand is secure for the future.

Things have certainly changed from 1957 when the Massey Ferguson name was first used on the 35 and 65 tractors as well as the combines, balers and other equipment produced then. Many factories have closed in that time, but the Beauvais facility remains as a cornerstone of the AGCO brand in Europe and continues to produce red- and grey-painted tractors bearing the Massey Ferguson name, sixty years after that name first graced the side of tractor bonnets!

A Massey Ferguson 25 meets a Massey Ferguson 6499 – both were built in the same factory in Beauvais in France.

A superb stand put together at a show in Norfolk by dealers Thurlow Nunn Standen and consisting of a Morris Minor service van plus a 35X and 65 representing the first phases of the MF tractor and a brand-new 7726 model from the current range. Together they represent sixty years of tractor development and the story that has been told in this book.